MW00444635

This Book Belongs To

____

Dates

__________ to __________